Discovering Religions

Buddhism

Sue Penney

Dec '03

Heinemann Educational Publishers
Halley Court, Jordan Hill, Oxford OX2 8EJ

OXFORD MELBOURNE AUCKLAND
JOHANNESBURG BLANTYRE GABORONE
IBADAN PORTSMOUTH NH (US) CHICAGO

First published 1988
Revised edition published 1995

03 02
10

British Library Cataloguing in Publication Data
A catalogue record for this book is available from the British Library

ISBN 0 435 30469 0

Designed and typeset by Visual Image
Illustrated by Visual Image
Produced by Mandarin Offset
Printed in Great Britain by Bath Press Colourbooks, Glasgow

Acknowledgements

Religious Studies consultant: W Owen Cole

Thanks are due to Anil Goonewardene for reading and advising on the manuscript.

The publishers would like to thank the following for permission to use photographs: Andes Press Agency p. 42; Aspect Picture Library p. 37; Christophe Bluntzer/Impact Photos p. 20; The Bridgeman Art Library pp. 28, 29; The J Allan Cash Photo Library pp. 13, 22, 25, 33; Circa Photo Library pp. 19, 43; Bruce Coleman Ltd p. 6; Douglas Dickins pp. 10, 30; C M Dixon p. 23; Anil Goonewardene p. 27; Sally and Richard Greenhill p. 47; Robert Harding Picture Libary pp. 31, 32, 35; Graham Harrison pp. 17, 18, 40; The Hutchison Library pp. 26, 46; Barry Lewis/Network p. 11; G Mermet/Impact Photos p. 44; Christine Osborne Pictures p. 45; Pana/Press Association p. 36; Ann and Bury Peerless pp. 8, 9, 38; Still Pictures p. 14; Topham Picturepoint p. 21; Zefa Pictures pp. 24, 34.

The publishers would like to thank the Hutchison Library for permission to reproduce the cover photograph.

The publishers have made every effort to trace copyright holders. However, if any material has been incorrectly acknowledged, we would be pleased to correct this at the earliest opportunity.

Contents

MAP: where the main religions began

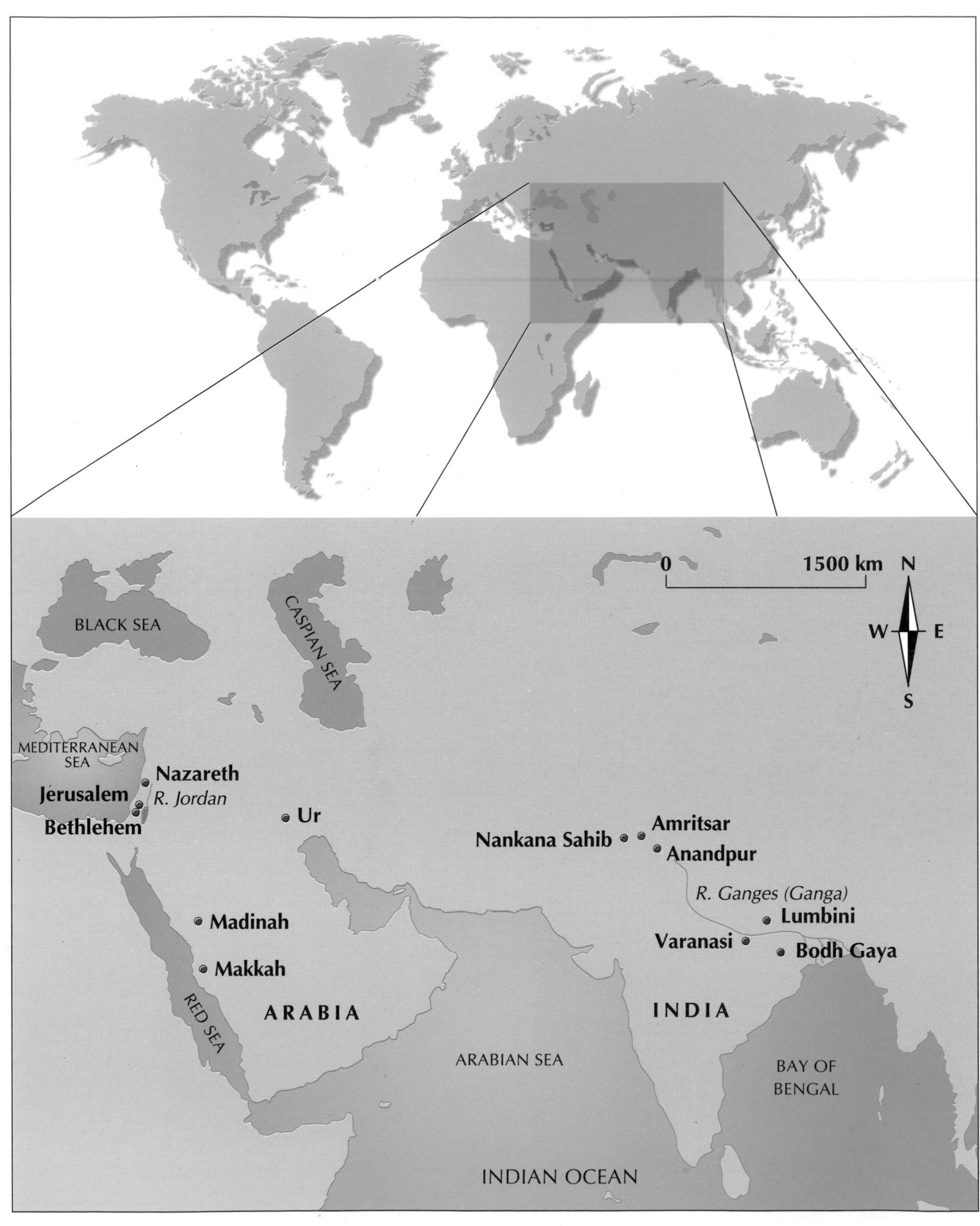

TIMECHART: when the main religions began

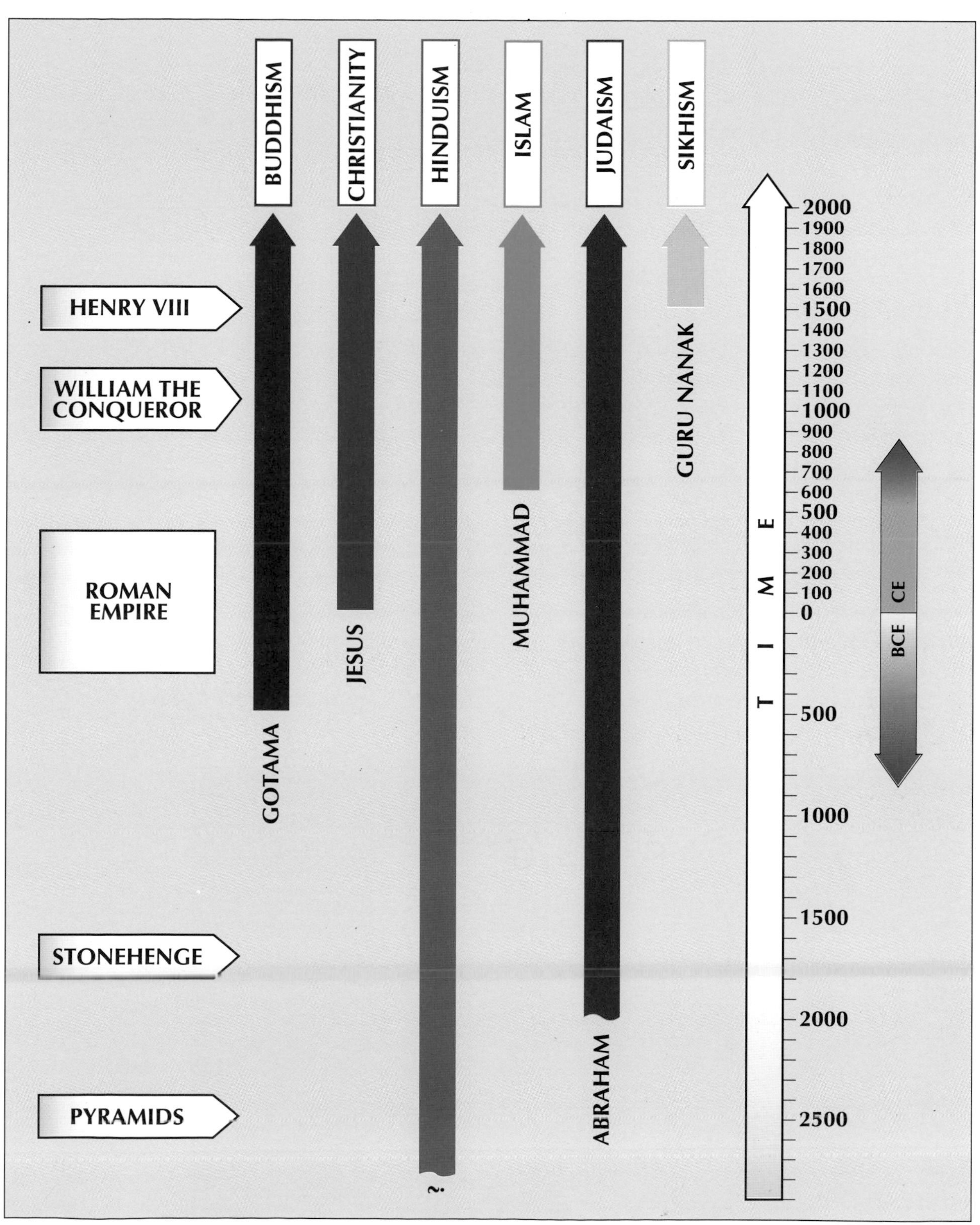

Note about dating systems

In this book dates are not called BC and AD which is the Christian dating system. The letters BCE and CE are used instead. BCE stands for 'Before the Common Era' and CE stands for 'Common Era'. BCE and CE can be used by people of all religions, Christians too. The year numbers are not changed.

Introducing Buddhism

This section tells you something about who Buddhists are.

The present Buddhist teaching began in India about 2500 years ago. Today, there are estimated to be about 327 million Buddhists, most of whom live in Asia. There are about 130,000 Buddhists living in Britain.

What do Buddhists believe?

Buddhists follow the teachings of a man called Siddattha Gotama, the **Buddha**. He lived in India in the sixth century BCE. Buddha is not a name, it is a special title. It means someone who has gained **Enlightenment**. Enlightenment is a special understanding – realizing the truth about the way things are. Buddhists believe that everything in the world is imperfect. They believe that in his Enlightenment the Buddha found the answer to why this is so, and how it can be overcome. They believe that by following the teachings of the Buddha, other people can gain Enlightenment, too. Buddhists do not believe in an all-powerful God, and they do not believe that the Buddha himself was more than a human being. He was important because he achieved Enlightenment, and chose to teach others the way to achieve it, too.

Buddhists believe that unless they gain Enlightenment, when they die each person will be reborn. This belief is called **samsara** – a continual round of birth, old age, illness, death and 'rebecoming' or rebirth. Buddhists aim to break out of this continuous cycle and achieve **Nirvana**. (This is sometimes spelt **Nibbana**.) Nirvana is the end of imperfection. Buddhists say that it is the 'blowing out of the fires' of greed, hatred and ignorance, which is followed by a state of perfect peace. They try to reach Nirvana by following the Buddha's teachings, and by **meditation**. Meditation means training your mind so that you can concentrate more fully. By meditating, Buddhists aim to control their mind so that they can go 'beyond' thought. This is explained in more detail on page 22.

The lotus is a symbol of things which are pure and good

Symbols of Buddhism

The **symbol** used for Buddhism is a wheel. This has eight spokes, which is a reminder that part of the Buddha's teaching was about eight ways of living. (This is explained in more detail on pages 16–17.) The wheel itself is a reminder of the continual cycle of birth, death and rebirth, which goes on and on like a wheel turning.

The symbol of Buddhism

Another symbol which Buddhists often use is the **lotus** flower. It is a symbol of things which are pure and good. A lotus is a sort of water lily. It begins its life in the mud at the bottom of a pond, and rises to the surface of the water to flower. The flower is not spoiled by the mud in which it grows. Buddhists say that in the same way, people can rise above the things which are not satisfactory in life, and achieve Enlightenment.

New words

Buddha 'the Enlightened one'
Enlightenment understanding the truth about the way things are
Lotus flower which looks like a water lily
Meditation mental control leading to concentration, calmness and wisdom
Nirvana (Nibbana) the stopping of greed, hatred and ignorance
Samsara continual round of birth, illness, death and rebirth
Symbol something which stands for something else

Test yourself

What does Buddha mean?

What does Enlightenment mean?

What's meditation?

What's a lotus?

Things to do

1 Explain why a wheel is one of the symbols of Buddhism.

2 What is samsara? Why do Buddhists believe that this is so important?

3 Use the picture to help you draw a lotus flower. Write a paragraph explaining why Buddhists believe that the lotus can be a symbol.

4 Find out more about when Buddhism began and where most Buddhists live. (The map and timechart at the beginning of this book will help, so will books in the library.) Write a short article explaining what you have found out.

The life of the Buddha

This section tells you about the life of Siddattha Gotama, the Buddha.

Siddattha's early life

Siddattha Gotama was an Indian prince. He was born at Lumbini, in what is today called Nepal, in the fifth century BCE. The stories say that when Siddattha was born, his father asked eight wise men what he would become. All of them agreed that he would be a great man, but they said that if he ever saw suffering, he would become a great religious leader rather than a great ruler. Siddattha's father ordered that no one who was sick or old should be allowed near the prince. Siddattha grew up to be handsome and clever. When he was sixteen he married a beautiful girl, and they had a son. Siddattha was rich and powerful – it seemed that he had everything he could want.

However, Siddattha became bored with his sheltered life in the palace, and one day he went riding outside the palace grounds. While he was out, four things disturbed him very much. He saw an old man – he had never seen old age before. He saw a sick man – he had never seen illness before. He saw a funeral, with the relatives weeping around the body. He had never seen sorrow or death before. As he was thinking about these things, he saw a holy man. The man was contented and happy, and said that he had given up his home and his family to wander from place to place searching for the answers to the problem of suffering in the world.

Siddattha was deeply disturbed by what he had seen, and decided that he, too, must try to find the answer to this problem. He left the palace that night, changed his royal robes for the simple clothes worn by holy men, and shaved his head.

Siddattha's search for Enlightenment

For the next six years, Siddattha travelled around India. He spent some time with two great teachers, then with a group of **monks**. He spent several years with five holy men who lived a very hard life, eating and drinking almost nothing. The idea was that if you force your body to suffer, it becomes less important to you. He found that starving himself did not help him to find any answers, so he began eating and drinking again. The holy men left

This old painting shows Siddattha leaving his palace

The Mahabodhi temple at Bodh Gaya

him in disgust, because they thought he had given up. Siddattha travelled on until at last he came to a great tree. Today this is called the **bodhi tree**, which means 'tree of wisdom'. He sat under the tree and meditated, and at last he gained Enlightenment. In other words, he achieved understanding of the meaning of life. Buddhists say that this is a feeling of total peace, when you can stop thinking about yourself and become totally free.

From this time on, Siddattha Gotama was called 'the Buddha'. According to Buddhist teaching, having achieved Enlightenment, Siddattha could have left Earth, but he chose not to do this. He believed that his knowledge should be passed on to others, so he spent the rest of his life teaching other people about the right ways to live. He passed away (Buddhists do not say that he died) at the age of 80. His body was **cremated**, and the ashes were placed in special burial mounds called **stupas**. Buddhists say that the Buddha's passing away was when he entered **Parinirvana**. This is the name given to the 'complete' Nirvana at the end of a Buddha's life.

New words

Bodhi tree the 'tree of wisdom' under which the Buddha achieved Enlightenment
Cremate burn a body after death
Monk man who dedicates his life to his religion
Parinirvana complete Nirvana
Stupa place where part of the Buddha's ashes were buried

Test yourself

Where was Siddattha born?

What's a monk?

What's Parinirvana?

Things to do

1. What were the four things which Siddattha saw outside the palace? Why did they disturb him so much?
2. Explain why the monks lived such a hard life. Why do you think they were so disgusted with Siddattha when he gave up their way of living?
3. How could meditation help Siddattha to find the answer to the meaning of life?
4. Draw a series of pictures to show important events in the life of Siddattha Gotama. Use these words as titles: Prince, Meeting suffering, Meditating, Teaching.

Buddhist teachings

This section gives you an outline of Buddhist teachings.

The Three Jewels

Buddhist belief is summed up in the words which Buddhists repeat every day:

> *I take refuge in the Buddha*
>
> *I take refuge in the **Dhamma** (teaching)*
>
> *I take refuge in the **Sangha** (Buddhist community)*

These are called the Three Jewels because they sum up the most precious part of Buddhist belief. The Buddha is respected because he showed the way to Enlightenment. The Dhamma is respected because Buddhists believe that the teaching needs to be realized in your own life. Today, 'Sangha' means the Buddhist monks and **nuns** who offer help and guidance in following Buddhism. A refuge is a safe place, so when Buddhists say that they 'take refuge' in these three things, it is a way of showing how important they are.

Dhamma

The Buddha's teachings are the most important part of Buddhism. Buddhists do not believe that the Buddha 'invented' the teachings, because they believe that they are natural laws which have always existed. (The word dhamma means 'natural law'.) They do believe that the Buddha was the person who put the teachings in a form that can be understood by people in this age of the world. Buddhists believe that by following the teachings and realizing that they are true for themselves, they can achieve Enlightenment themselves.

Enlightenment

Enlightenment means 'realizing the truth'. It is not the same as knowing things, because knowledge can be taught. Enlightenment is different, because each person has to find the truth for themselves. (It may help you to understand this if you think of learning to swim or ride a bicycle. You can be told what to do, and understand what to do, but you have to discover the knack for yourself.) Buddhists believe that when they reach Enlightenment, they can break free of the endless round of birth, illness, death and rebirth. They can enter Nirvana.

Girls worshipping at a temple in Burma

Buddhists at a monastery in Scotland

Nirvana

Buddhists say that it is not possible to describe Nirvana. There is a Buddhist story about a fish and a turtle who were friends. The fish asked the turtle to describe what life was like on land. The turtle tried, but the fish could not imagine air or trees or grass or anything else which the turtle was talking about. Buddhists say that trying to describe Nirvana is like this. The only way is to say what it is not like. Nirvana really means 'going out' – like a fire goes out because it has no fuel. It is not life, it is not death. It means being free of greed and anger, and the end of everything that is imperfect. It is the state where 'you' does not exist any longer. For a Buddhist it is the only way to be really free.

New words

Dhamma 'natural laws' – teachings of the Buddha
Nun woman who dedicates her life to her religion
Sangha community of Buddhist monks and nuns

Test yourself

What's the Sangha?

What's a nun?

What's a refuge?

Things to do

1 Explain why the three most important Buddhist beliefs are called the Three Jewels.

2 What does dhamma mean? Why do the Buddha's teachings have this name?

3 Why is reaching Enlightenment so important for Buddhists?

4 Working in pairs, imagine the conversation between the turtle and the fish about what life is like on land. Write up what you talked about. What other things can you think of which are important even though they are difficult to explain? (**Clue**: hope? fear? ambition? feelings?)

Teachings of the Buddha I

This section tells you about part of the Buddha's teachings.

After the Buddha's Enlightenment, many people came to listen to him teaching, and became his followers. He taught for nearly 50 years before he passed away, and his teaching was passed down by his followers who learned it off by heart. People in those days were used to learning things, because not many people could read or write, and this was the usual way to pass on important teachings. The Buddha's teaching was about all areas of life, but it is usually agreed that it is summed up in three parts. These are called the Three Signs of Being, the Four Noble Truths, and the Noble Eightfold Path. Buddhists believe that together these three show the way to live. They are not separate ways to choose – they all depend on each other, and need to be followed all together. This section looks at the Three Signs of Being.

The Three Signs of Being

The Three Signs of Being are **dukkha**, **anicca** and **anatta**. They are three of the most important words in Buddhist belief.

Dukkha

Dukkha is often translated 'suffering', but it means much more than pain. It means things like being uncomfortable or bored, too. Everything that is unsatisfactory is dukkha. Buddhists believe that this means life is dukkha, because there is nothing in life that is absolutely perfect. The Buddha said that no one can escape dukkha. His teaching was a way of overcoming it.

Anicca

Anicca means 'impermanence' – in other words, nothing lasts. People, plants, even 'solid' things like mountains are changing all the time. The Buddha said that because nothing remains the same for long, there is no rest except Nirvana.

Anatta

Anatta means 'no-soul'. The Buddha taught that there is nothing which can be called a soul. Instead, he said that people are made up of five parts. They have a body, they can feel things, they have ideas, they can think and they can be aware of things going on around them. These five things make up each person.

This teaching was particularly important, because it is connected to another Buddhist belief – the teaching about rebirth. All Buddhists believe in rebirth – the continual round of birth, illness, death and rebirth called samsara – but they do not believe that a soul or spirit continues from one body to another.

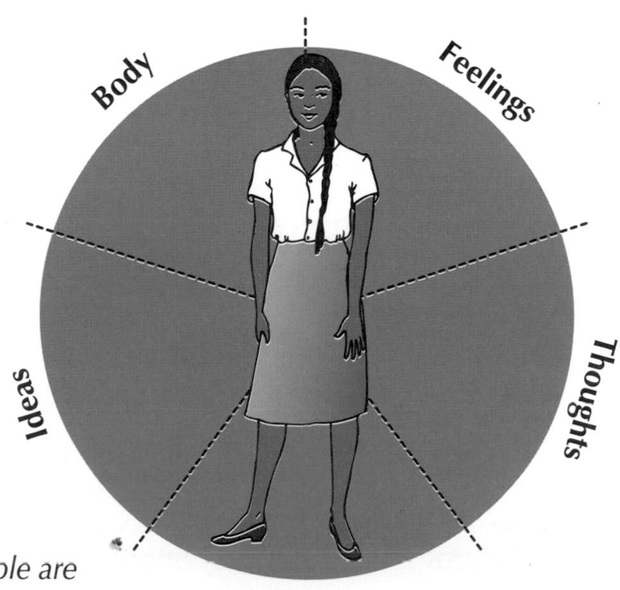

The Buddha taught that people are made up of five parts

Worshippers at a temple in Thailand

Instead, they say that what continues is the 'life-force' which the person has made by the actions they have chosen in their life. Actions are called **kamma**, and the Buddha taught that each person's kamma affects their future lives. The 'force' of a good life this time means they will be reborn into a 'higher' life next time. A bad life means that they will be reborn into a 'lower' life next time. All previous lives have an effect. Buddhists believe that the only way to break out of the force of kamma is to follow the Buddha's teachings, and to meditate.

New words

Anatta belief that there is nothing which can be called a soul

Anicca 'impermanence' – belief that nothing lasts

Dukkha suffering, and everything that is unsatisfactory

Kamma actions which affect future lives

Test yourself

What are the three parts of the Buddha's teachings?

What does anicca mean?

What does anatta mean?

What does dukkha mean?

Things to do

1 How were the Buddha's teachings first passed on? What are the advantages and disadvantages of this method?

2 Why is dukkha such an important word for Buddhists? What reason did the Buddha give that life was dukkha?

3 Explain the Buddha's teaching about what makes a person.

4 What do you think about the idea that actions in this life can affect your future life? What difference do you think it would make to the world if everyone believed this?

Teachings of the Buddha II

This section tells you about the Four Noble Truths.

Most Buddhists would agree that the Four Noble Truths are the most important part of the Buddha's teaching. It was the main part of the first teaching he gave after his Enlightenment. He taught about the causes of dukkha (things being imperfect), and how it can be overcome. He said that when people realized the Four Noble Truths, they would be able to change their lives.

Buddhists say that all life is dukkha

The First Noble Truth

Dukkha happens everywhere all the time.

The Buddha said that everything in the world is dukkha, because nothing is perfect. Every life has the kamma (force) from the person's previous lives, and so being reborn means that everyone always suffers from the force of their previous lives. This means that every life has something wrong with it. Only when people have reached Nirvana will they be able to overcome dukkha.

The Second Noble Truth

Dukkha is caused by greed and selfishness.

Everybody is basically selfish. We all tend to think about ourselves more than others, and we are always more concerned with what we want to do than with what other people want to do. This selfishness is a cause of the suffering in the world. The Buddha said that even being reborn is really selfish, and people should try to break out of the rebirth cycle.

The Third Noble Truth

Greed and selfishness can be stopped.

When you no longer want anything – when you can see beyond yourself, and what you are is no longer important – then you can leave suffering and imperfection behind. A Buddhist believes that you can only do this by breaking out of the rebirth cycle, which brings perfect freedom. This freedom is Nirvana.

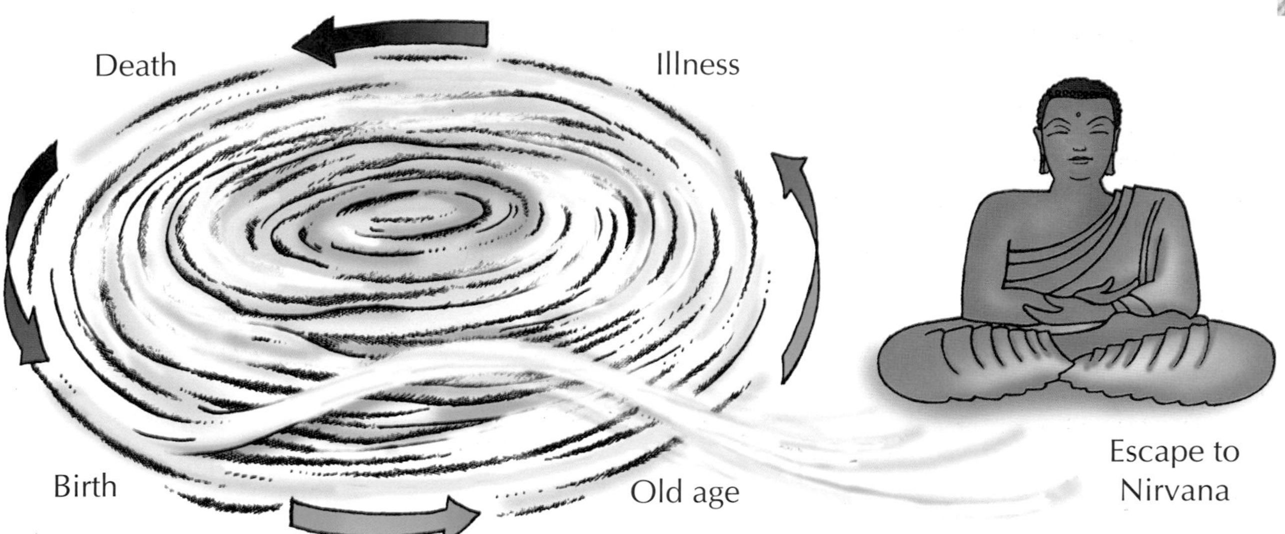

The cycle of life

The Fourth Noble Truth

The way to stop selfishness is to follow the Noble Eightfold Path.

The Noble Eightfold Path is sometimes called the 'Middle Way'. It is the way of living which the Buddha said led to Nirvana. It is a way of helping people to realize Nirvana by showing them how they should live. The Buddha said that it was as if people were trying to walk through very muddy ground. They can only be helped out of it by people who are standing on firm ground. The Noble Eightfold Path is the way to find this firm ground.

Test yourself

How many Noble Truths are there?

How can dukkha be overcome?

How can selfishness be stopped?

Things to do

1 Put the Four Noble Truths into your own words, and explain why they are so important for Buddhists.

2 Why do you think the Buddha taught that being reborn is basically selfish?

3 The Buddha's teaching was that selfishness leads to suffering. Write a story which shows that this is true.

4 Draw a diagram or picture to show how Buddhists aim to break out of the cycle of birth and suffering. (Use the drawing on this page to help you, if you wish.)

Teachings of the Buddha III

This section tells you about the teachings called the Noble Eightfold Path.

The Buddha said that people should follow a 'Middle Way' to Nirvana. You should not live a life of luxury where you over-eat and have too much of everything. But equally you should not live a life where you starve yourself and punish your body. People who do these things will not find Nirvana. The secret is to follow a middle path between extremes.

The Noble Eightfold Path

The path which the Buddha taught about is called the Noble Eightfold Path. As its name suggests, it shows eight ways in which people should live. All of these things need to be acted on together – there is no point in following just one or two of the ways. All the parts of the path begin with the word 'right'. This does not only mean the correct way to do something. It also means the best possible way. The eight parts of the path are usually put into three groups. The first two parts go together.

Right viewpoint

A viewpoint is a way of looking at things. Unless you look at life in the right way, you will not be able to reach Nirvana. This means following the basic teachings of Buddhism, for example, accepting that all of life is unsatisfactory (dukkha).

Right thought

Your mind is very powerful, so it needs to be used in the right way. Thinking correctly about life leads to you being unselfish and caring about others rather than concentrating on yourself.

The next three ways show how Buddhists should behave when following the Path.

Right speech

Right speech does not cause harm to yourself or others. You should be kind and helpful when you talk to people, and not tell lies, swear or gossip.

The Noble Eightfold Path

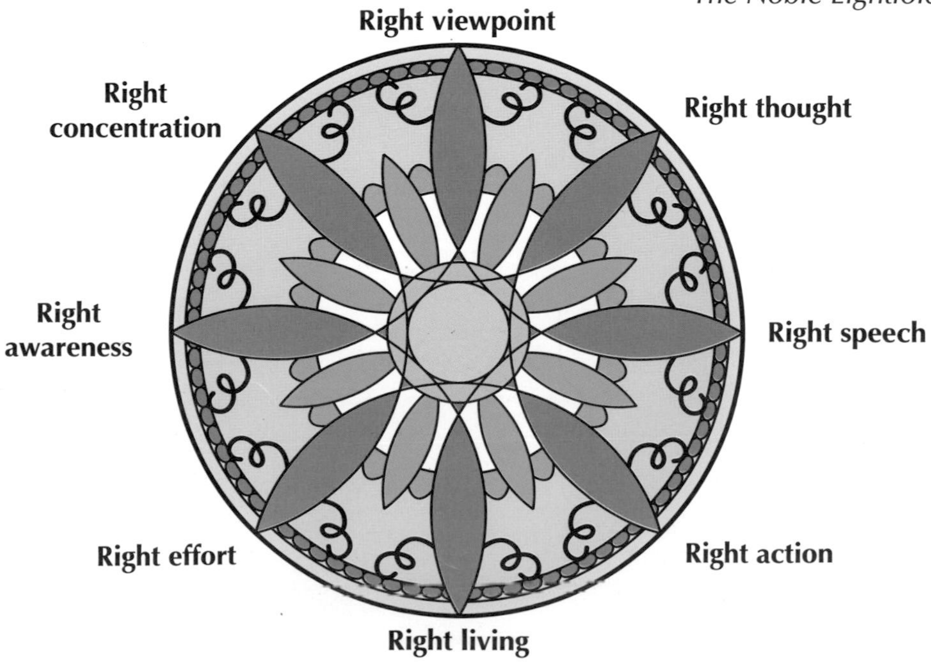

Lighting candles is part of Buddhist worship

Right action

Right action includes avoiding killing anything, and avoiding stealing or being dishonest. It also includes being faithful to your husband or wife, and not drinking alcohol or taking drugs, because these things are harmful.

Right living

Someone who wants to follow the Buddha's teachings should work to the best of their ability. The job you do should be useful, and not involve anything which harms others.

The next three ways are about training the mind.

Right effort

Training yourself to avoid bad things is part of right effort, but a Buddhist must also work hard to do good.

Right awareness

This means controlling your mind so that you can see things around you in the right way.

Right concentration

Training your mind to concentrate without wandering is achieved by meditation. When you can do this, you will become a very calm and peaceful person.

Test yourself

What does 'right' mean in the Noble Eightfold Path?

Where does the Noble Eightfold Path lead?

Things to do

1 Explain what the Buddha meant when he talked about a 'Middle Way'. Why do you think he thought this was so important? (Look back at the section on The life of the Buddha, on pages 8–9, to help you.)

2 Why do you think training your mind by meditation can help you to reach Nirvana?

3 The Buddha's teaching about right living includes working hard but not harming others. What sort of jobs do you think a Buddhist should avoid?

4 Do you think it would be easy to follow the Noble Eightfold Path? Write about the things in yourself which you would need to change.

Theravada and Mahayana

This section tells you about the two main groups of Buddhists.

All Buddhists follow the teachings of the Buddha, but like most religions, different groups do not agree exactly about their beliefs and the way in which things should be done. In Buddhism, groups are known as 'schools'. There are two main schools. One is usually called **Theravada** Buddhism, the other is usually called **Mahayana** Buddhism. Both of these schools have within them smaller groups who emphasize particular ideas or beliefs.

Theravada Buddhists

Theravada means 'teachings of the elders'. Elders are respected leaders of a religion. Theravada Buddhism is based on Buddhist teachings which were written in the language called **Pali**. Theravada is sometimes called 'southern' Buddhism because it is mainly found in countries like Sri Lanka, Burma, Cambodia, Thailand and Vietnam.

Theravada Buddhists emphasize the idea that each person must gain Enlightenment for themselves. No-one else can do it for you. They believe that the Buddha taught people how they should live, but he was only a man. The only way he can help people to gain Enlightenment today is through his teachings, so Theravada Buddhists do not pray to the Buddha.

Theravada Buddhists think that the best way to live is as a monk or a nun. Monks and nuns can concentrate on their religion, because they have no responsibilities like a family or possessions. Not everyone can leave their home and dedicate their life to religion, and Theravada Buddhists accept that this means monks and nuns may be closer to Nirvana than other people.

Mahayana Buddhism

Mahayana Buddhism began in India in about 100 BCE. It is now more popular in the 'northern' countries of China, Japan, Korea and Tibet and includes many different schools of Buddhism. Mahayana Buddhism uses the same ideas as Theravada Buddhism, but in some cases it has changed the way they are understood and explained. Mahayana means 'great vehicle'. This is a way of saying that there is room for different ways to Nirvana. Mahayana Buddhists believe that anyone can reach Nirvana if they follow the Buddha's teachings, and ask him for help.

Theravada Buddhist monks in Burma

Buddhism

An image of the Bodhisattva Kuan Yin

One of the ways which Mahayana Buddhism is most different is the belief in **Bodhisattvas**. A Bodhisattva is someone who has reached Enlightenment, and so could enter Nirvana. Instead, they have chosen to be reborn and stay in the world to help others to achieve Enlightenment, too. There are many thousands of Bodhisattvas. Mahayana Buddhists pray to them for help in achieving Enlightenment, and also for help with problems in everyday life.

Test yourself

Where is Theravada Buddhism most common?

Where is Mahayana Buddhism most common?

What's Pali?

Things to do

1 Why do you think that there are different schools of Buddhism?

2 Explain why Theravada Buddhists think that being a monk or nun is the best way to live.

3 What is a Bodhisattva? Explain why Mahayana Buddhists pray to Bodhisattvas.

4 Choose Theravada or Mahayana Buddhism, and find out more about one of the countries where it is practised. Geography books and books in the library will help. Put together a short project showing how Buddhism affects life in the country you have chosen.

New words

Bodhisattva person who has reached Enlightenment but has chosen to be reborn to help others
Mahayana 'great vehicle' (school of Buddhism)
Pali ancient language
Theravada 'teachings of the elders' (school of Buddhism)

Other schools of Buddhism

This section tells you about three of the best-known smaller schools of Mahayana Buddhism.

Zen Buddhism

Zen is a Japanese word which means meditation. Zen Buddhism is most popular in Japan and Korea, and in China where it is called Cha'an.

Like all Buddhists, followers of Zen Buddhism aim to reach Enlightenment. Buddhists say that you cannot reach Enlightenment by thinking about it – you have to go 'beyond' your mind to achieve it. Zen Buddhists have their own ways of trying to reach Enlightenment, and say that it comes as a flash of higher understanding.

Like other Buddhist monks, Zen monks live in **monasteries**, but their training is usually more strict than other monks' training. They meditate for several hours each day in a special room, using ways of meditating which are special to Zen. They meditate sitting in the lotus position (cross-legged with each foot resting, sole up, on the opposite thigh). One of the best-known parts of Zen meditation is the use of 'koans' – meditating on statements which do not seem to make sense. One of the most famous koans is 'Imagine the sound of one hand clapping'. The idea is to cause your mind to leave its usual ways of thought, to 'shock' it into understanding.

Pure Land Buddhism

Pure Land (Jodo Shu) Buddhism is a school of Mahayana Buddhism which is particularly popular in Japan. It says that the age of the world in which we live is so wicked that people cannot achieve Nirvana on their own. The only hope is to pray to the Buddha Amida who is Lord of the Pure Land. This is a stage on the way to Nirvana. A **mantra** used by followers of this school is 'Nembutsu Amida' which means 'I call on you, Amida'. The ideas of the Pure Land school are not accepted by many other Buddhists, who feel that they do not follow the teachings of the Buddha Gotama.

The garden is an important part of a Zen monastery

Tibetan Buddhism

The branch of Buddhism which developed in Tibet has many different parts. Tibetan Buddhists respect the Dalai Lama. They believe that he is an appearance of the Bodhisattva who is most important for Tibetans. There is a mantra which is like a prayer to this Bodhisattva. It is '*Aum mane padme hum*'. In English this is 'Glory to the jewel in the lotus' but its true meaning cannot really be translated. This prayer and others are written on prayer wheels and prayer flags. A prayer wheel is a cylinder with prayers written on the outside or on paper rolled up inside it. The larger the wheel, the more powerful the prayer. Many temples have prayer wheels bigger than a person. As the wheels are turned and the flags blow in the wind, Tibetan Buddhists believe that the prayers are repeated over and over again. The prayers are a way of building up **merit**, which is the reward for doing good things. It helps you on your way to Nirvana.

Prayer wheels and prayer flags at a temple in Nepal

New words

Mantra sacred chant which Buddhists believe has special power
Merit reward for good actions
Monastery place where monks live

Test yourself

What's a monastery?

What's a mantra?

Where is Pure Land Buddhism most popular?

Things to do

1. Explain what Zen Buddhists hope to achieve by their meditation.
2. Why do you think that some Buddhists feel that the teachings of Pure Land Buddhism do not follow the teachings of the Buddha?
3. Why do Tibetan Buddhists turn prayer wheels and put up prayer flags?
4. Find out more about the Dalai Lama. Where does he live? Why? Why is he so important for Tibetan Buddhists? (Books on Buddhism will help, and you may be able to find articles in newspapers.) Write a short article explaining what you have found out.

Worship I

This section tells you about how Buddhists worship.

'Worship' often means praying to a God or gods, and for this reason many Buddhists do not like using the word. In this book, worship means Buddhists meditating and reading from the holy books.

Buddhists may worship on their own or in groups. There is no special day of the week when they meet for worship, but days before the moon is new, full or at half-moon are important.

Meditation

Meditation

For most Buddhists, meditation is the most important part of worship. They usually sit on the floor, often with crossed legs, and try to empty their mind of all thoughts. This means that they can begin to focus on things that are really important. The point of meditation is to 'rise above' any worries you may have, and the world and its problems. It is intended to control and develop the mind. By meditating, Buddhists believe that they will become better people, and will be able to achieve Enlightenment.

Group worship

When Buddhists meet for worship, it is usually in the **shrine**-room of a temple. The shrine is beautifully decorated, and contains an **image** of the Buddha. An image of the Buddha is called a **Buddharupa**. Before they go into the shrine-room, worshippers will remove their shoes. Inside, there are no seats, so worshippers sit on the floor. Legs are kept crossed or pointing to one side, as it is not thought to be respectful to point the legs towards the image. Worshippers may greet the Buddharupa by putting their hands together in front of their chest or face, and bowing slightly. This is the usual way of greeting anyone in many Eastern countries. Sometimes a Buddhist may touch their chest, lips and forehead with their hands, to show that their body, their speech and their mind are all joining in the greeting. They may bow or kneel, and sometimes lie flat on the floor. These are all ways of showing respect to the image.

The people offer gifts of flowers and light (by lighting candles or lamps). In a temple, monks usually carry out the formal parts of the ceremonies. The people watch and meditate, and repeat set words and chants after the monks. There are readings from the Buddhist holy books, and a senior monk often gives a talk. At the end of the ceremony, the people often stay and drink tea together. Tea-drinking ceremonies can be part of worship as well as a way of getting rid of thirst. People sit quietly, drinking specially prepared tea from beautiful crockery. There are often flower arrangements. The idea is to be surrounded by peace and beauty.

Individual worship

When they worship on their own, Buddhists meditate and repeat important parts of the holy books. Usually these are chanted – a special sort of singing using only a few notes. They often burn **incense**, and offer flowers and sometimes food like grains of rice to the Buddharupa. They may light candles, which are a symbol to show the light of the Buddha's teaching. Theravada Buddhists do not pray as part of their worship, but part of Mahayana Buddhist worship is to pray to Bodhisattvas for help in their lives.

Gifts may be offered to the Buddharupa as part of worship

New words

Buddharupa image of the Buddha
Image statue
Incense sweet-smelling perfume
Shrine holy place

Test yourself

What's a shrine?

What's an image?

What's a Buddharupa?

What's incense?

Things to do

1 How many things can you list which show that Buddhists treat the shrine with respect?

2 Explain why tea-drinking ceremonies can be part of Buddhist worship.

3 Using information in this and other units, imagine you have been to a Buddhist meeting. (Go to a real one if you can!) Write a letter to a friend describing what happened and your impressions.

4 Working in small groups, discuss how meditation might help you to become a better person. Write up your conclusions.

5 What special movements can you think of which people use in ordinary life to show respect?

Worship II

This section tells you about the places where Buddhists worship.

Shrines

A shrine is special to followers of the religion, and Buddhists usually worship in front of a shrine. Shrines are beautifully decorated, and contain an image of the Buddha, a Buddharupa. They also contain holders for incense, and usually flowers and candles. There are also places where offerings can be left. Different Buddhist schools have different traditions about other things which may be found in shrines – for example, Zen Buddhist shrines may have offerings of tea, Tibetan Buddhist shrines have bowls of water in them.

A Japanese Buddhist woman worshipping at the shrine in her house

Shrine-rooms may also be quite different. In Zen Buddhism, rooms are usually very plain and simple. In some other traditions they may be quite highly decorated. A shrine may be in a monastery or temple, or it may be one room in an ordinary house. This is more likely in Britain and other countries where there are not many Buddhist temples.

Monasteries

A monastery is a place where monks live. Buddhist monasteries are 'open', because the monks do not live apart from ordinary people. Many Buddhists who live near a monastery go there to worship and study. For many children, the monastery is also their school, where they are taught to read and write by the monks. Some Buddhist monasteries are just one building, but most are like a small village. The most important room is the shrine-room, which is used not just for worship but for all important meetings of the monks. There are also huts where the monks live. This is explained in more detail on pages 40–1.

An important part of a Buddhist monastery is the garden. Many monasteries have a well-planned garden, with trees and shrubs. The trees give shade, which is important in hot countries, and the gardens help to make the monastery a place of peace and quiet. The plants are also symbols that nothing lasts, because they grow, die and their seeds grow again. In countries where it is possible for them to grow, monastery gardens often include a bodhi tree. This is the tree under which the Buddha was sitting when he achieved Enlightenment, so Buddhists think bodhi trees are important.

The stupa at Bodnath, in Nepal. (The eyes are symbols of the all seeing eyes of the Buddha)

Stupas

Many Buddhists go to worship at important stupas. A stupa is a burial mound. Some are part of monasteries, but others are built at holy places. After the Buddha had passed away, his body was cremated, and the ashes were taken to eight different places. Stupas were built around them. Another two were built, one over the spot where the body had been cremated, and one where the container used to collect the ashes was buried. Ten stupas therefore contain remains of the Buddha. Later, many other stupas were built where people wished to honour 'special' Buddhists.

Test yourself

What do shrines contain?

Why is the bodhi tree important?

What's a stupa?

Things to do

1 What sort of things might you find in a Buddhist shrine? Explain why these things are placed there.

2 Why do many Buddhist children learn to read and write in monasteries?

3 Explain why the garden can be such an important part of a Buddhist monastery. What do the plants symbolize?

4 Why were stupas built? Why do you think many Buddhists go to visit them?

Holy books

This section tells you about the holy books of Buddhism.

At first, none of the Buddha's teachings were written down. People in those days were used to remembering important teachings. However, soon after he had passed away, people began to think that it would be a good idea to make sure there was a clear record of what the Buddha had said. This was because his teachings were thought to be so important. A special meeting of 500 Buddhist monks was arranged. All the Buddha's teaching was recited by the **Venerable** Ananda and the Venerable Upali, who were two of the Buddha's closest followers. All the monks repeated the teaching together. This made sure that everyone agreed.

This teaching was passed down by the monks. It was not written down for about 400 years, but in that time there were several meetings to check that it was still accurate and to organize it. The two most important collections of the Buddha's teaching are the Pali **Canon** and the **Sanskrit** Canon. They are called this because Pali and Sanskrit are the ancient languages in which they were first written, and canon means 'collection of writings'. The fact that Buddhist Scriptures are written in two languages is the reason why many important Buddhist words can be spelled two ways – for example, Nirvana and Nibbana. Nirvana is the Sanskrit form, Nibbana is the Pali form. Neither form is better or more correct than the other. The Pali Canon was the first collection to be written down. It is also called the **Tipitaka**, which means 'three baskets'. It was probably given this name because the teachings were first written down on palm leaves, which were kept in baskets. The Tipitaka are the most important teachings for Theravada Buddhists.

Reading and learning the holy books is important

The Tipitaka

The first 'basket' of the Tipitaka is called the Vinaya Pitaka, which means 'discipline'. It contains the rules for monks to follow, with some stories and other teachings. The second basket is the **Sutta** Pitaka, which contains most of the dhamma, the teachings of the Buddha. The most well-known part of this basket is called the Dhammapada. The third basket is the Abhidhamma Pitaka, which means 'higher teaching'. It mainly contains writings which explain the Buddha's teaching.

The most important of these three is the Sutta Pitaka, because it contains the teachings of the Buddha. A sutta is a small piece of teaching. The Sutta Pitaka also contains stories about the Buddha, including stories about his previous lives before he was Gotama. The most important part is the section called the Path of Teaching, because this contains the Four Noble Truths and the Noble Eightfold Path.

Buddhist nuns in Britain reading from the holy books

Mahayana Buddhist books

Mahayana Buddhists also follow the teachings of the Tipitaka, but they do not agree with Theravada Buddhists about which teachings are the most important. Two of the most important teachings for Mahayana Buddhists are the Diamond Sutta and the Lotus Sutta. Mahayana Buddhists also have their own special texts.

New words

Canon collection of writings (the Buddha's teaching)
Sanskrit ancient language
Sutta small part of teaching, usually the Buddha's
Tipitaka 'baskets' – collection of the Buddha's teaching
Venerable term of respect used for Buddhist monks

Test yourself

What does Venerable mean?

What's Sanskrit?

What's a sutta?

Things to do

1 Why were the holy books of Buddhism written down?

2 **a** Explain why the Tipitaka has this name.
b What does it contain?
c What is the most important part?

3 Diamonds and lotuses are beautiful. Why do you think Mahayana Buddhists gave these names to two suttas?

4 Using information from this book and any other books you can find which contain Buddhist teaching, work in groups to make a wall display by writing out Buddhist teachings. You could call it 'The Second Basket'.

Symbols in Buddhism

This section tells you about some of the symbols which Buddhists use.

Like all religions, Buddhism includes many ideas which are difficult to explain. Using symbols helps to make things clear without having to use words. The lotus flower, for example, is often used as a symbol for Buddhism (see page 7). Flowers may be used as offerings at Buddhist shrines. They help to make the shrine attractive and they smell pleasant, but they are also a symbol of the belief that everything is dukkha, because they die quickly.

The Buddha

Images and pictures of the Buddha often use symbols. There are thousands of images of the Buddha, and he is usually shown in one of three positions – standing, sitting or lying down. If he is standing, he usually has one hand raised, as if he is blessing people. If he is sitting down, he is often shown meditating in the lotus position. If he is shown teaching, he is usually sitting with one hand raised. Sometimes the first finger of his left hand is pointing to his right hand, and the thumb and first finger of his right hand form a circle. This is called 'Setting the Wheel of Law in motion'. It is a reference to his first teaching, when he talked about the laws of life. When the right hand is shown touching the Earth, it is a symbol that he is calling on the Earth to take notice of his teachings. This refers to a story about his Enlightenment. Pictures and images of him lying down usually show him at the end of his life just before he entered Parinirvana.

Whatever the position, pictures and images of the Buddha may show any or all of 32 special symbols which show that he was not an ordinary person. For example, there is usually a 'bump' on the top of this head, which is a sign that he had special gifts. He is often shown with a round mark on his forehead, which is sometimes called a third eye. No one suggests that Gotama really had this, but it is a symbol that he could see things which ordinary people cannot see. He is usually shown with long ear lobes, which is a sign that he came from an important family. His hair is usually curled, a symbol that he was a very holy man.

This image of the Buddha shows several of the special features

A mandala

Mandalas

A **mandala** is a specially designed pattern, made up of circles, squares and triangles. Sometimes mandalas are just patterns, but others include pictures of the Buddha or of Bodhisattvas. The Wheel of the Law (the wheel with eight spokes which shows the Noble Eightfold Path) is one of these mandalas.

Another important mandala comes from Tibetan Buddhism. It is the Wheel of Life. It is made up of several pictures in a circle. The monster which holds the circle is the Lord of Death. The outside ring shows the twelve stages that human beings go through from birth to death. Inside this is a series of pictures showing possible places of rebirth. In the centre are three animals – a snake, a cockerel and a pig. These are symbols – the snake stands for hatred, the cockerel for greed and the pig for ignorance. Pictures like these show Buddhist teachings and are used to help Buddhists meditate.

New word

Mandala specially designed pattern

Test yourself

What are flowers a symbol of?

How many symbols can be used in images of the Buddha?

What's a mandala?

Things to do

1 Why do you think Buddhism uses so many symbols?

2 Explain why pictures and images of the Buddha need to show that he was not just an ordinary person.

3 What can mandalas be symbols of? Why are wheel shapes likely to be popular with Buddhists?

4 Draw your own picture of the Buddha showing the symbols, or one of the other symbols mentioned in this section. Explain what symbols your picture shows.

Pilgrimage

This section tells you about important places which Buddhists visit.

Many Buddhists feel that it helps them to follow their religion if they visit places where the Buddha lived and taught. They may also visit places like the stupas where parts of the Buddha's ashes were buried. Journeys which are made for reasons like these are called **pilgrimages**. People have many different reasons for going on pilgrimages, but for Buddhists the main reason is that they believe going to holy places, especially places where the Buddha lived and worked, will help them in their own search for Enlightenment.

Places where the Buddha lived

The Buddha was born in a place called Lumbini, in what is now called Nepal. The site where he was born is marked by a simple stone pillar which says on it 'Here the Buddha was born'. This is now quite a difficult place to get to, but a small group of monks live there, and there are temples where people meditate.

Bodh Gaya is the place in India where the Buddha gained Enlightenment. Buddhists from all over the world visit it, and it is an important meeting place. A bodhi tree grows there which is said to be descended from the very tree under which the Buddha sat to meditate. Pilgrims walk around this tree, their heads and feet bare as a sign of respect. They often sit under the tree to meditate, and offer flowers and other gifts. There are many temples nearby, and places where pilgrims can stay.

Other places of pilgrimage

The Buddha passed away at Kushinagara in northern India, and many Buddhists visit the

The Shwe Dagon temple in Burma

Sunrise at Sri Pada

stupa there. There are stupas in most Buddhist countries, but some of those in India, Nepal and Sri Lanka are the most important, and many Buddhists make pilgrimages to them. When visiting a stupa, a Buddhist walks around it at least three times. This remembers the Three Jewels (the Dhamma, the Buddha and the Sangha). Some temples are built where there are remains of the Buddha. The Shwe Dagon temple in Burma, for example, has eight of the Buddha's hairs. In Sri Lanka, there is a festival every year in the town of Kandy, where one of the Buddha's teeth is kept in the Temple of the Sacred Tooth (see page 34).

Some mountains are very important for Buddhists. One of the most important is Sri Pada, on the island of Sri Lanka. Buddhists believe that the Buddha visited Sri Lanka three times, and went once to Sri Pada. At the top of the mountain is a stone which has what looks like footprints on it. Buddhists believe that these footprints were left by the Buddha.

New word

Pilgrimage journey made for religious reasons

Test yourself

What's a pilgrimage?

Where did the Buddha pass away?

Where's Sri Pada?

Things to do

1. Explain why Buddhists go on pilgrimages.
2. Why is Bodh Gaya a particularly important place of pilgrimage?
3. Why do Buddhists walk around a stupa three times?
4. **a** Imagine you are a Buddhist on a pilgrimage. Write a postcard to friends at home, telling them what you have seen and what you have been doing.

   b Use one of the photos in this book or another picture of your choice to draw the picture for your postcard.

Festivals I

This section tells you about festivals in Thailand, a Theravada Buddhist country.

Buddhists live in many countries. They follow the same religion, but of course groups of Buddhists also keep many of the customs of the country where they live. This means that the same festival can be celebrated in quite different ways in different countries.

Songkran

In Thailand, the festival of Songkran takes place in April and lasts for three days. It is the Thai New Year. Buddhists go to the local monastery to give presents to the monks. These are things like flowers, food and candles. Everyone eats special foods, and wears new clothes. This is a symbol that the new year is a chance to make a fresh start.

Water is important in the festival of Songkran. Boat races are held on rivers, and there are often water fights in the streets. During the dry season, fish are often trapped in ponds which form when the smaller rivers dry up. These fish are rescued by the people and kept until Songkran, when they are released into the deep river. Sometimes caged birds are set free instead. These customs are to follow the Buddha's teaching about being kind to all living things. Buddhists believe that by setting the creatures free, they will gain merit (see page 21).

Songkran ends at midnight on the third day. In temples and monasteries all over Thailand, a drum is beaten and a bell rung at the same time. This is repeated three times. When the sound has died away, the festival is over.

Wesak (called Vaisakha in some countries)

Wesak is celebrated by Buddhists all over the world. In Britain it is sometimes called Buddha Day. It celebrates the three most important events in the Buddha's life – his birth, his Enlightenment and his passing away.

Celebrating Songkran

Theravada Buddhists believe that these three events all happened on the day of the full moon in the month of Wesak (May or June in the Western calendar), so this is the date the festival is held. Many Buddhists give each other cards and presents to celebrate the festival.

In Thailand, people visit the temples and monasteries at Wesak. The monks give talks and preach to the people about the life of the Buddha. The shrines in the temples are beautifully decorated, and the people pour scented water over the image of the Buddha, the Buddharupa. At night, the image is taken out of the temple and put on a special platform. People walk around it carrying lamps, so that the Buddharupa is surrounded by light.

Pouring scented water over the Buddharupa

Kathina

Kathina is a Thai festival which takes place at the end of the rainy season (November in the Western calendar). It is a time when people can take gifts to the monastery, to say 'thank you' to the monks for the work they do during the year. It also shows that the people realize how important the monks are. The gifts are useful things like cloth for new robes. No monk is allowed to own things himself, so the gifts are given to the monastery. Giving at this time is thought to earn more merit for the giver.

Test yourself

How long does Songkran last?

What are the other names for Wesak?

When does Kathina take place?

Things to do

1 Why do people set fish and birds free at Songkran?

2 **a** Why do you think that people pour scented water over the Buddharupa at Wesak?
b Why do you think they surround the Buddharupa with light?

3 Why do people give gifts to the monastery at Kathina?

4 Find out more about Buddhism in Thailand. Do a project with pictures – you could choose to concentrate on one of the famous temples. Geography books will help, and a travel agent may be able to give you leaflets which you could use.

Festivals II

This section tells you about festivals in Sri Lanka.

Wesak

As in Thailand, the most important festival in Sri Lanka is Wesak, when Buddhists remember the three most important events in the Buddha's life. In Sri Lanka, special ceremonies and worship take place in the temples. Streets and houses are lit with lanterns and there are plays and dancing to celebrate the festival. Everyone makes a special effort to be kind to other people, and some people set up stalls by the side of the road, offering free food and drink to passers-by. This is to remind everyone what the Buddha taught about being kind to others.

Poson

Poson is the month which falls in June-July in the Western calendar. The festival – also called Poson – is held on the day of the full moon. It celebrates the time when Buddhism was first brought to Sri Lanka in 250 BCE. Buddhists believe that the first Buddhist missionaries to go to Sri Lanka were a monk and a nun who were the son and daughter of the Emperor Asoka (see page 38). They were called the Venerable Mahinda and the Venerable Sanghamitta. A special play is performed in the town of Mihintale, where they arrived.

Esala Perahera

In the town of Kandy in Sri Lanka there is a Buddhist temple which was specially built to keep a **relic** of the Buddha – one of his teeth. This is kept locked away in a special **casket**, but for ten days every August the festival of Esala Perahera is held in its honour.

The most important part of the festival is a procession lit by torches, which takes place on

Esala Perahera

Dancing is an important part of many festivals

the night of the full moon. Over a hundred elephants take part in this procession. They are beautifully decorated, and wear brightly coloured cloths. The most important elephant, called Jayarajah, carries a special casket. This is an exact copy of the one which holds the Buddha's tooth. (The real one is far too important to be taken out of the temple.) Other elephants carry caskets with relics of other important Buddhists. The procession travels through the town, watched by huge crowds. This is a religious festival, but it is also a time for enjoying yourself, and there are dancers, drummers and fire-eaters. People light fireworks and burn incense and other sweet-smelling perfumes. Many people go to Kandy to watch the procession and to join in the festivities.

New words

Casket special container
Relic object which is old and treasured (usually remains of a holy person)

Test yourself

When was Buddhism brought to Sri Lanka?

What's a relic?

What's a casket?

Things to do

1. Explain why Wesak is the most important festival. What are the celebrations in Sri Lanka?
2. Why do you think Sri Lankans celebrate Poson?
3. How many reasons can you give why relics of the Buddha are so important?
4. Imagine you have watched the Esala Perahera procession through Kandy. Write a newspaper article with a picture, telling your readers what it was like.

Festivals III

This section tells you about some of the most important festivals in Japan.

Japan is a Mahayana Buddhist country. This means that many of the festivals are different from those in Theravada Buddhist countries, although some still celebrate the same important events.

New Year

The Japanese use the same calendar as people in Western countries, so New Year falls on 1 January. For Japanese Buddhists, the day before is more important. This is when the 'Evening Bells' ceremony takes place. At midnight, the bells in every Buddhist temple are struck 108 times. This is a special number for Buddhists, because many Buddhists believe that it is the number of 'mortal passions' – things like envy and jealousy. They believe that each ring of the bell drives out one of these faults. This is a time when Buddhists think about the things which have been wrong with their lives in the past year, and what they can do to improve their lives in the new year.

Obon

Obon takes place for four days in July. It is a family festival and, if possible, people go home to their parents to celebrate it. The festival remembers one of the old stories about the Buddha. The story says that the mother of one of the Buddha's followers was rescued from hell by the Buddha. Some versions of the story say that the Buddha used a rope to pull her out, so in some places the festival is celebrated by tug-of-war competitions.

Mahayana Buddhists believe that the Buddha can help you in your life, and asking for his help is one of the purposes of this festival. They also believe that it is important to ask for his help for members of the family who have died. People visit the graves of relatives. In some areas, it is thought that the spirits of people who have died come back to the family home, so lamps are lit to show them the way.

Obon is a serious festival, but it is also celebrated with fairs and dancing. One particular dance where everyone joins hands and dances round in a circle gives the festival its name.

Ringing the bell at a temple

Visiting the graves of relatives who have died is an important part of some festivals

Higan

Higan takes place twice a year at the times of the equinoxes. These are the two occasions during the year when day and night are of equal length. It is also the time when the seasons begin to change. This is a sort of symbol, because it reminds Buddhists that they need to change their lives so they can reach Enlightenment. Higan is a time for remembering friends and relatives who have died. Buddhists go to the **cemeteries** to clean and look after the graves, and decorate them with flowers. There are special ceremonies which they believe give merit to people who have died. This is important, because they believe the extra merit can help them on their way to Nirvana.

New word

Cemetery place where dead bodies are buried

Test yourself

Which Buddhist school is mainly followed in Japan?

Where does the name Obon come from?

Things to do

1. Why do Mahayana Buddhists think it is important to pass on merit to people who have died?
2. Why do you think some Buddhists believe that spirits may come back to the family home at Obon?
3. Why might New Year and the equinoxes be times when people think about changes they need to make in their lives? Is having a special time for thinking about this a good idea? Give reasons for your answer.
4. Obon and Higan are both festivals when relatives who have died are remembered. Why do you think this may be important for Buddhists?

The history of Buddhism

This section tells you something about the history of Buddhism.

The present Buddhist teaching began in India, when Siddattha Gotama began teaching. He had reached Enlightenment, but chose to stay in the world to show others the best way to live. His first followers were the five holy men who had spent years with him when he was still searching for Enlightenment. Before long, other people became interested in his teachings, too, and asked to join him. The group became known as the Sangha. This name is still used, but today it is used to refer to Buddhist monks and nuns. The Buddha's first followers included his own son, Rahula. At first, women were not allowed, but after he had been persuaded by his stepmother and his cousin, the Buddha agreed that women, too, could join the group. For the next 45 years, the Buddha spent his time travelling around India and neighbouring countries, preaching and teaching.

Emperor Asoka

After the Buddha had passed away, his followers carried on his teaching, and Buddhism continued to grow. The teaching about respecting all life caught the attention of the Emperor Asoka. He had fought many successful wars, and ruled almost the whole of India from 273 BCE to 232 BCE. He became unhappy at the suffering and death caused by the wars he had fought, and **converted** to Buddhism. He tried to rule according to Buddhist teachings. He encouraged other people to become Buddhists, and sent monks and nuns travelling from place to place teaching about Buddhism. Among these preachers were his own son and daughter, who took the teachings of Buddhism to Sri Lanka. Asoka ordered that stone pillars should be put up at places where important things had happened to the Buddha, with writing on them explaining what they were, and he suggested that people should go on pilgrimages to these places. He also had his policies for government written up in the same way. Many of these writings still survive today.

The spread of Buddhism

As Buddhism spread, different groups began to emphasize different teachings. This led to the development of the two main groups of Buddhists which still exist today, Mahayana and Theravada Buddhism. As Buddhism spread to

A stone pillar from the time of Asoka

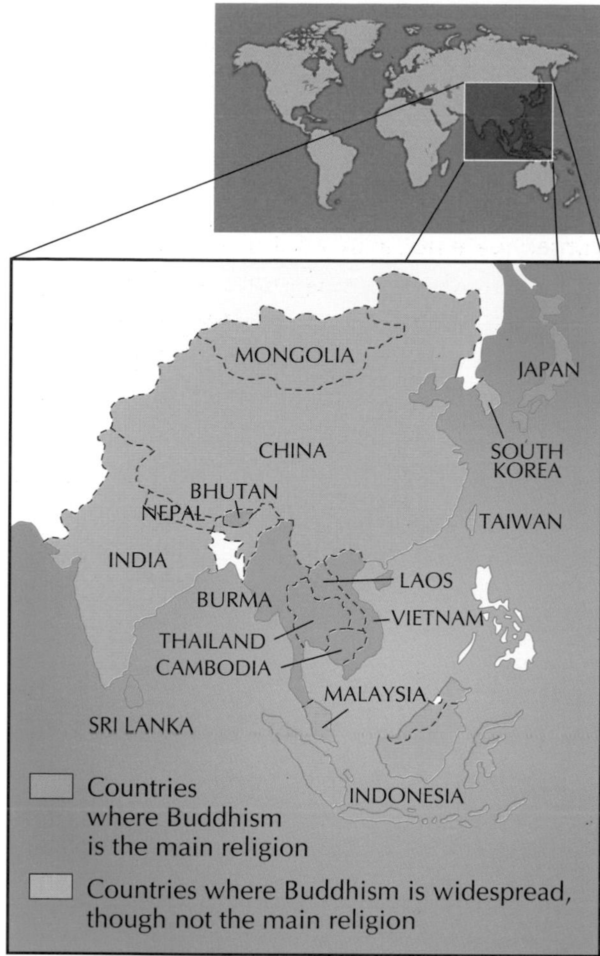

Buddhism in the world today

different countries, people who became Buddhists did not leave behind everything they had known before. This means that Buddhist customs and particularly festivals may be quite different in different countries.

Numbers of Buddhists

Some 'Buddhist countries' are ruled by governments that do not approve of the teachings of Buddhism, and this makes it difficult to know how many Buddhists there are in the world. It is also hard to estimate because many Buddhists do not attend temples, but have shrines in their homes. In 1991, the official figure was estimated to be 327 million, but other people suggest that the true figure may be nearer to 600 million.

New word

Convert become a member of a religion

Test yourself

How long did the Buddha preach for?

When did the Emperor Asoka live?

What are the two main groups of Buddhists?

Things to do

1 How do you think the five monks felt when they became the Buddha's first followers? What changes would they have needed to make to their lives? (Look back at the section on the Buddha's life on pages 8–9 to help you.)

2 Explain why the Emperor Asoka became a Buddhist.

3 Buddhism spread very quickly. How many reasons can you give why this happened?

4 Imagine you are one of the early Buddhist monks. How would you start to tell people about the Buddha's teaching?

5 How easy or difficult do you think it would be to become a follower of a new religion?

Buddhist monks and nuns

This section tells you something about Buddhist monks and nuns.

A Buddhist monk's work is his religion. Many Buddhist men become monks for a few months or years, so that they have time to study and learn about their religion. It is not expected that all monks will stay in the monastery all their lives. Especially in Theravada Buddhist countries, it is common for young boys to become monks so that they can be educated in the monastery. They may leave when they become adult. Women may become nuns, but this is not as common. Nuns and monks live in the same way, although the rules they follow are not always exactly the same. This section concentrates on monks because there are many more Buddhist monks than nuns.

A Buddhist monastery has small huts where monks live alone. The huts are furnished very simply, with a mat which is the monk's bed, and a small table or stool. He is expected to sit on the floor. There may also be a small shrine to help the monk meditate. Anything which is not essential – for example, pens and paper or books – are the property of the monastery, not his own. The only things which a monk owns himself are the robes he wears – most monks have two – and a few necessary items. These are needle and thread to repair the robes, a razor, because most monks shave their heads, a bowl and cup for food and drink, and a special strainer. This is to remove any insects from his drinking water. The Buddha taught his followers to be kind to all living things, and this means that Buddhists try hard not to kill anything, even by accident.

Buddhist monks spend most of the day alone, studying and meditating, but there is usually a time when they meet to study and meditate together. The Buddha taught that it is important to help others, and many monks spend part of their day working to help other people. This may be teaching, giving advice to people who need it, or some other form of service. As part of their simple life, their main meal is always eaten before midday, and after this time all monks **fast** until the following morning, although they may drink water, or tea without milk or sugar.

A Thai Buddhist monk studying outside his hut

Alms

Monks are given their food and everything else they need by people living around the monastery. This is not begging, because Buddhists are pleased to give to the monks. It is called giving **alms**. Buddhism teaches that giving to others is very important, and giving to monks is part of a Buddhist's religious duty. It also helps to earn merit. It used to be the custom for monks to go out on an alms round every morning, but today it is more usual for people to bring their gifts to the monastery.

The five precepts

All Buddhists are expected to follow the five **precepts**, which are the 'guides' for living as a Buddhist. A precept is a rule or guide to show you how to live. The five precepts are:

- not to harm living beings
- not to take what is not given
- to avoid improper sexual activity
- not to take part in improper speech
- to avoid alcohol and the misuse of drugs.

When a Buddhist becomes a monk or nun, these rules are followed more strictly – for example, all sexual relationships are forbidden, and a Buddhist monk should not even be alone in the same room as a woman. There are also five extra precepts which all monks and nuns and some Buddhists who are not monks or nuns choose to follow. They agree not to:

- eat after midday
- attend music or dancing
- use perfume or jewellery
- sleep on a soft bed
- accept gifts of money.

There are also rules of the monastery which monks and nuns must keep. The rules tend to be more strict in Theravada Buddhist countries.

New words

Alms giving food and necessary things
Fast do without food and drink for religious reasons
Precept rule or guide for living

Test yourself

What are alms?

What's a fast?

What's a precept?

Things to do

1 Explain why Buddhists are pleased to give alms to the monks.

2 Why do you think some people who are not monks or nuns may choose to live according to the 'extra' five precepts?

3 What reasons can you give why a Buddhist boy might join a monastery for a few years?

4 Find out more about the life of Buddhist monks and nuns. Books about Buddhism in the library will help, and there may be information in books about Buddhist countries.
   a Write about a day in the life of a Buddhist monk (or nun if you prefer).
   b Draw a picture which shows something about the monk's or nun's life.

Buddhism in Britain

This section tells you about Buddhism in Britain.

Until about a hundred years ago, Buddhism was almost unknown in Britain. The first Buddhist missionary to teach in Britain arrived in 1893. In 1901, an Englishman called Alan Bennett travelled to Burma to become a Buddhist monk. He took the name Venerable Ananda Metteya, and returned to Britain in 1908. He spent the rest of his life spreading the message of Buddhism in Britain. The Buddhist Society of Great Britain and Ireland was formed at this time. As travel has become easier, more people have visited countries where Buddhists live, and knowledge has increased. Some people have become attracted by Buddhist teaching, and have become Buddhists themselves.

Some converts say that they like Buddhism because it does not ask them to believe anything they have not thought out for themselves. Others find that they agree with its teaching about the importance of taking care of everything in the world. Buddhism teaches about caring, not only for other people, but also for animals, insects and the earth itself.

Buddhist monks and nuns in Britain

Most Western Buddhists do not become monks and nuns, but there are a few places in Britain where Buddhist monks and nuns live. They live in much the same way as they would in Buddhist countries, spending their time meditating and teaching. They live very simply, and most do not have any belongings of their own. Some do not handle money. It is usual for Buddhists to take food and other necessary things to the monastery. 'Alms rounds' are not usual in Britain.

Retreats

Many Buddhists who are not monks or nuns go to the monasteries on **retreats**. A retreat is a special time when you leave your normal life behind for few days or weeks. Buddhists on

Inside the Buddhapadipa temple in London

The Samye Ling Tibetan monastery in Scotland

retreat spend a lot of time meditating. A retreat in a monastery gives people the chance to be with other Buddhists and to live like a monk for a short time. They believe that this makes them better Buddhists in their everyday lives.

In 1991 there were estimated to be 130,000 Buddhists living in Britain. There are several different groups of Buddhists, whose teachings are slightly different. Many Buddhists say that it is important to join a group whose teachings you agree with. The largest number of Buddhists follow Theravada teachings. The next most popular is the Tibetan and then the Zen tradition. There are also groups which aim to combine the most important teachings of Buddhism with Western ways of living. Most groups have temples, and worship is the same as it would be in a country where most people are Buddhist. People go there to meditate and listen to talks by the monks. There is no fixed day for worship in the temple, but Sunday is often popular, because it fits into the usual way of British life.

New word

Retreat special time of meditation away from normal life

Test yourself

When did the first Buddhist missionary come to Britain?

What's a retreat?

About how many Buddhists live in Britain?

Things to do

1 Why have many Western people become interested in Buddhism?

2 Explain why many Buddhists find that going to monasteries on retreat is useful.

3 Why might a Buddhist monk or nun find life in Britain difficult?

4 See if you can talk to a Buddhist about their beliefs and their life in Britain. Use what they tell you to write a short project called 'Buddhism in Britain'. If you cannot find someone to talk to, use a library to find as much information as you can in books.

Special occasions I

This section tells you about some important ceremonies for young Buddhists.

Most religions have teachings about birth and death, but Buddhism teaches that the way you live is far more important. There are very few teachings in Buddhism about the beginning and ending of life because of the Buddhist belief that there is no soul. This means that – from the point of view of belief – birth and death are not very important. For most people, however, births and deaths are a very important part of life, and many Buddhists follow the customs of their country. This means that Buddhists in different countries may have quite different **rituals**. This section looks at the customs in Burma and Thailand, which are Theravada Buddhist countries.

Birth

The birth of a new baby is a time for happy celebrations. In countries like Burma and Thailand, it is the custom for the oldest members of the family to prepare gifts for the baby. A cradle is made ready, with clothes for the baby in it. When the baby is placed in the cradle for the first time, the gifts are placed around it. The gifts are usually 'useful' things – if the baby is a boy, they may be tools and books. For a girl, they are more likely to be needles and threads.

The head shaving ceremony

The main ceremonies happen when the baby is a month old. The head is shaved, because the hair is seen as a symbol of a bad kamma in a previous life. Sacred threads are tied around the baby's wrists. Monks are often invited to this ceremony and they may be asked to suggest a name for the baby. Food is always given to the monks when a baby is born.

Joining a monastery

Many Buddhist boys join a monastery at least for a few months. This often happens when they are in their teens or their early twenties, but in Burma and Thailand almost all boys join

A Buddhist monk school in Thailand

Many Buddhist boys enter a monastery to be taught by the monks

when they are ten or even younger. A boy who joins the monastery at this age is not expected to stay there all his life. Many boys stay for a short time, from a few weeks to a few years, so that they can be educated by the monks.

The **ordination** ceremony when a boy becomes a monk is one of the most important Buddhist ceremonies. In Burma, the boy acts out the story of how Siddhatta Gotama left his comfortable palace and became a wandering monk. There are special ceremonies, the boy's head is shaved (most monks have shaved heads), and older monks help him to dress in the monk's robes.

New words

Ordination ceremony in which a person becomes a monk
Ritual usual 'pattern' for ceremonies

Test yourself

What's a ritual?

When does the head shaving ceremony take place?

What's ordination?

Things to do

1 Why does Buddhism not have many teachings about birth and death?

2 Explain the reasons why a baby's head is shaved.

3 Why do you think a monk may be asked to suggest a name for the baby?

4 How many reasons can you think of why joining the monastery is such an important ceremony for young boys?

5 Imagine you are a Buddhist child joining a monastery. Write a letter home telling your friends about your first day. (Look back at the section on Buddhist monks on pages 40–1 to help you.)

Special occasions II

This section tells you about Buddhist ceremonies for marriage and death.

Marriage

In most Buddhist countries, marriages are arranged by the parents of the couple. This is because they have had more experience of life, so are thought to know best. It is also because marriage joins two families, so it is thought that the families should be involved in the decision. The parents usually arrange for their son or daughter to meet a suitable person. The couple have the right to say 'No', but if they agree to the marriage, astrologers (people who tell the future from the stars) will usually be asked to suggest a good date for the wedding to take place.

A Buddhist wedding in Malaysia

In Buddhist countries, the wedding usually takes place in the bride's home. The ceremony is usually performed by a male relative of the bride, rather than a monk. The couple stand on a special platform called a **purowa**, which is decorated with white flowers. They usually exchange rings, and the thumbs of their right hands are tied together. Sometimes their right wrists are tied together with a silk scarf, instead. This is a symbol that they are being joined as husband and wife. Children recite particular parts of the Buddhist holy books, and the couple repeat promises that they will respect and be faithful to each other.

A monk may give a talk about the Buddha's teaching on marriage as part of the wedding. If this does not happen, it is usual for the couple to go to the monastery together before or after the wedding, and listen to the Buddha's teaching there. At the end of the ceremony, everyone shares a meal. The celebrations after the wedding may go on for several days.

Death

Buddhist funerals are dignified, but they are not sad events, because of the idea that the person will be reborn. A monk may give a talk about the Buddha's teaching on what happens after death, and the Five Precepts and the Three Jewels are repeated. The body is usually cremated, and the ashes are scattered or buried.

When someone dies, their relatives often give gifts to the monks. They ask that the merit they gain from doing this should be shared with the person who has died. They believe that this may help the person. For the same reason, Buddhists always look after graves very

Buddhist monks at a funeral ceremony in Singapore

carefully. At festivals every year, there are ceremonies to 'pass on' merit to the person who has died. Some Buddhists believe that there are places where a person can 'rest' between lives, so passing on merit to them will help in their next life.

New word

Purowa special platform for marriage

Test yourself

Who is usually in charge at a Buddhist marriage ceremony?

What's a purowa?

What is repeated at a Buddhist funeral?

Things to do

1. Explain the symbols which show that the couple are being joined in marriage.
2. Why do the relatives of someone who has died give gifts to the monks?
3. Why do you think the Five Precepts and the Three Jewels are repeated at a funeral service?
4. Design a card which would be suitable to send to a Buddhist couple on their wedding day.

Glossary

Alms giving food and necessary things
Anatta belief that there is nothing which can be called a soul
Anicca 'impermanence' – belief that nothing lasts

Bodhisattva person who has reached Enlightenment but has chosen to be reborn to help others
Bodhi tree the 'tree of wisdom' under which the Buddha achieved Enlightenment
Buddha 'the Enlightened one'
Buddharupa image of the Buddha

Canon collection of writings (the Buddha's teaching)
Casket special container
Cemetery place where dead bodies are buried
Convert become a member of a religion
Cremate burn a body after death

Dhamma 'natural laws' – teachings of the Buddha
Dukkha suffering, and everything that is unsatisfactory

Enlightenment understanding the truth about the way things are

Fast do without food and drink for religious reasons

Image statue
Incense sweet-smelling perfume

Kamma actions which affect future lives

Lotus flower of the water lily family

Mahayana 'great vehicle' (school of Buddhism)
Mandala specially designed pattern
Mantra sacred chant which Buddhists believe has special power
Meditation mental control leading to concentration, calmness and wisdom
Merit reward for good actions
Monastery place where monks live
Monk man who dedicates his life to his religion

Nirvana (Nibbana) the stopping of greed, hatred and ignorance
Nun woman who dedicates her life to her religion

Ordination ceremony in which a person becomes a monk

Pali ancient language
Parinirvana complete Nirvana
Pilgrimage journey made for religious reasons
Precept rule or guide for living
Purowa special platform for marriage

Relic object which is old and treasured (usually remains of a holy person)
Retreat special time of meditation away from normal life
Ritual usual 'pattern' for ceremonies

Samsara continual round of birth, illness, death and rebirth
Sangha community of Buddhist monks and nuns
Sanskrit ancient language
Shrine holy place
Stupa place where part of the Buddha's ashes were buried
Sutta small part of teaching, usually the Buddha's
Symbol something which stands for something else

Theravada teachings of the elders (school of Buddhism)
Tipitaka 'baskets' – collection of the Buddha's teaching

Venerable term of respect used for Buddhist monks